dear heart

dear heart

JENNY DAVIS

a sue hines book
ALLEN & UNWIN

First published in 1998
A Sue Hines Book
Allen & Unwin Pty Ltd
9 Atchison Street
St Leonards, NSW 2065 Australia
Phone: (61 2) 9901 4088
Fax: (61 2) 9906 2218
E-mail: frontdesk@allen-unwin.com.au
URL: http://www.allen-unwin.com.au

National Library of Australia
Cataloguing-in-Publication entry:
Brooks, Wynne.
Dear heart.

ISBN 1 86448 474 8.

1. Brooks, Wynne – Correspondence. 2. World War,
1939–1945 – Women – England – Correspondence.
I. Davis, Jenny, 1949– . II. Title.

940.548142

Designed & typeset by Ruth Grüner
Printed by Australian Print Group,
Maryborough, Victoria

3 5 7 9 10 8 6 4 2

Jacket photography: Christian Wild

p l a t e s

1 *Mickey and Wynne, 1940.*

2 *Mickey's first letter from overseas, 9 January 1942.*

3 *Harold (Mickey) Brooks.*

4 *Wynne's poem for Mickey's birthday, 18 March 1943.*

5 *Wynne Brooks.*

6 *Top: Mickey and Wynne, 1941.*

   Bottom: Returned letter, November 1945.

7 *Telegram from Air Ministry, 29 November 1945.*

8 *Wynne and Sidney Curtis, circa 1960.*

a c k n o w l e d g e m e n t s

There are a number of people who deserve my heartfelt thanks for their support and encouragement throughout this project, particularly my husband and family—and especially my daughter, Rebecca Davis, and her husband Stuart Halusz, for their moving creation of Wynne and Mickey/Sid on-stage in the first manifestation of *Dear Heart*, and my sisters Helen Reeves and Margaret Hobbs for their encouragement and research.

I would also like to thank Elvie Haluszkiewicz for her genially critical eye, Elizabeth Caiacob, Sally Tunnicliffe and Diana Denley for believing in *Dear Heart* the play and producing it in Perth, London and Sydney, Marty Lake, for his creative videotaping of the play, Selwa Anthony and Sue Hines, whose vision led to this publication, and Foong Ling Kong for her patient editing.

I wish I were able to thank those who inspired this story—my uncle and aunt, Sidney Curtis and Wynne (formerly Brooks), and, of course, Harold Brooks (Mickey), whom I never knew. I hope that they would approve if they were here to read this book.

author's note

This is a love story—the story of a young woman and a young man separated by thousands of miles and a barbed wire fence. Many lovers have been parted by war, many women have continued hoping when all hope was gone.

While the characters and most of the events in this story are true, I have taken the liberty of providing some of the details from my imagination. The letters are real, but since there are so many I have edited and amalgamated them and made some additions while remaining as true as possible to Wynne's voice.

Why were these lovers special? Because of the letters—and because all lovers are.

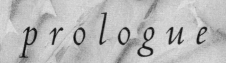

prologue

Essex

July 1988

The semi-detached brick villa was crowded with furniture. In the overstuffed sitting room photo frames ran amok on the piano and sideboard, and went on to decorate the window sills. It was a house in mourning, still echoing with the vibrations of its former occupants. Above in the attic, we sisters, inheritors of our uncle's estate, found boxes packed with ornaments from the fairground days of Aunt Wynne's youth.

We felt we knew Uncle Sid better than Wynne, who had died three years before. Sid was our father's brother and a great favourite of ours. We had been there for his last illness and loved him for his light-heartedness. Wynne we remembered fondly for her jollity and chatter—kneeling before her wardrobe, we had already smiled that day over her glass beads and dancing shoes, stroked her fur coat and amused ourselves over a collection of old theatre programmes. But we weren't prepared for the revelation in the attic that day, in the form of an old, battered suitcase. With the ignorance of youth we had always judged Wynne fun, but rather frivolous. We had known a little of her first marriage, but never equated the drama of her youth with the cosy and irrepressible Wynne of later years, never imagined the sensitivities that produced our discovery that day. As far as we knew, Wynne had never committed a word to paper. She communicated by telephone, and to me, who now lived in Australia, she and Sid never wrote, but sent cassette tapes talking, often both at once, of their evening classes, their dog, their amateur dramatics.

How little we know of others' lives—their passion, their loss, their courage. Enlightenment came that northern summer afternoon with that old suitcase, modest and unremarkable. It was only by chance that we even opened it, tired as we were and ready to consign much of the paraphernalia to the rubbish bin. We were mesmerised at first by the photos—a young man in uniform, a young woman with a smile to break your heart. And then we saw the letters, dozens of them, unopened, the paper yellowed but the ink still clear and inviting.

London
August Bank Holiday, 1939

It was an overcast day, and humid, but the few drops of rain in the afternoon had not deterred the holiday-makers from thronging to the fair. Wynne, whose father ran the fairground, was in charge of the tea tent—a warm occupation on a summer afternoon—serving doughnuts to children already pink and sticky from encounters with candy floss. Daphne, her hair in pins under her scarf, in order to be glamorous for a night out at the Ferry Boat, had already taken time off to nip home and cook her hubby's dinner, and Wynne had covered for her. Now it was Wynne's turn for a break, so as soon as there was a lull in business she left Daphne in charge and slipped out the back of the tent for a smoke.

It would have been a bit cooler outside, the air full of the scents and sounds of a London summer afternoon. Warm rubber on tarmac from the distant traffic, warm bodies jostling on the moth-eaten grass, the screams from the helter skelter and the big dipper, the pepper of shots from the rifle range, the 'Roll up! Roll up!' from across the ground at the coconut shy. Maybe Ronnie Smith, in shirt and braces, fingering the moustache he'd been trying to grow for a month, was helping the courting couples into the swing boats and hoping for a breeze to lift the girls' summer skirts. Wynne's friend, Vi, often teased her about the fairground boys. Wynne responded that they were a rough lot and she wouldn't dream of going out with them, but, nevertheless, she couldn't help enjoying the attention she received. She was, after all, a striking girl, a little vain of her curly dark hair and film-star red nails, and no doubt she was aware that Ronnie would be watching out for her.

But on this day someone else was watching, too. A tall young man in grey flannels was standing in the lee of the tent a few yards away. I'm sure

Wynne smiled at him, she was never without a smile. Tall men attracted her, but this one, regarding her so gravely, looked maybe a bit too serious. She was about to go inside when he came towards her, long legs stepping awkwardly over the guy ropes.

It was only a brief conversation. His name was Harold Brooks and he worked in the post office. He'd seen her in the pub but they hadn't been introduced. Vi had told him he'd find her here. He had appeared very intent and serious on that first meeting. Wynne was amused, and couldn't help teasing him a little. He had kind grey eyes; she wanted to make him laugh—she was a girl who liked to take the mickey—that's what she would call him, Mickey. As Wynne told it in later years, she was caught completely off-guard by his reply.

He said he would call her Mrs Brooks.

That evening in the pub, Daphne, her red curls carefully in place, was singing along with the piano. Eyes closed and a port and lemon in one hand, perhaps she was dreaming of the varnished hair and dark, liquid eyes of a Hollywood Valentino, and not of her old man propped at the bar with his cronies.

Wynne would have had to push through the crowd to reach her friends. Doreen, sitting on Stan's knee, was in high spirits. Next Saturday was her wedding day. She wanted to hear from Wynne about the recent modelling job at Liberty's. Did they want a good-looking blonde with short legs?

'Nothing wrong with short legs, is there Stan?'

'Ask me after next Saturday.' Full of beer and grins Stan and his mates slapped each other and shouted.

At the piano Daphne was imagining herself in a Fred Astaire and Ginger Rogers film, when Vi told Wynne that the new lad from the post office had just come in. Did she know he'd been asking after her?

A chorus of voices had joined Daphne's. It was a song that would grow in significance for Wynne and Mickey. 'The way you wear your hat, the way you sip your tea. The memory of all that, oh no, they can't take that away from me . . .'

Across the room he smiled at her at last. It was a smile that excluded everyone else. It would become her talisman.

⚜

Harold Brooks and Wynne were married during the blitz in an East London registry office in September 1940. It was a wartime marriage, no frills, with a few friends and family to help them celebrate in the pub, and a dash through the rain of bombs to their new home in Preston Road, Leytonstone. The austerity and dangers of wartime London could not blight their passion, but separation loomed from the start. As a civil servant, Mickey would not have been among the first to receive call-up papers, but by 1941 he was ACI Harold Brooks and stationed initially at

Blackpool, where Wynne took up lodgings to be near him and enjoyed their walks on the seafront and the camaraderie of other Forces' wives. Their first lengthy separation came with Mickey's transfer to an RAF camp in Scotland. Wynne returned home to Preston Road.

And so the letters began.

1941

To Mrs Wynne Brooks,
1, Preston Rd,
Leytonstone,
London E11

RAF Training, Lossie, Scotland
Dec. 4th 1941

Dear Heart,
Only a few days remain until we are together again.
That's the only thing I can think of, everything else
fades into the background. I'm so sorry this war has
kept us apart for our anniversary, but remember,
sweetheart, you are the centre of my being, without
you everything seems pointless and unreal. I feel so
helpless being up here when you are in the thick of
the bombing in London, and I worry about you
alone in the house. If there were to be an invasion as
they say, I think I would be so desperate I would
grow wings and fly just so I could be by your side.

I seem to be in the midst of an unhappy dream, where all the pleasant things of life are spoiled by the absence of some vital spark. You, my dear, are that vital spark, and I shall never be happy or fully alive so long as we are separated. I live for this weekend, London—and you.

Your own,
Mickey

It was frustrating for a young serviceman from London to be training in remote Scotland, only too aware that his loved ones at home were at the battlefront. But Mickey was soon to see action. In December 1941 he learned he was to be posted overseas and was given embarkation leave. He came home to their house in Preston Road for one precious, wet weekend shortly before Christmas.

Young Mr and Mrs Brooks went 'Up West' for a night on the town. Later, as the door of the restaurant closed behind them, they would have been plunged into the blackout, stumbling and laughing, the torchlight glistening on the wet pavement. (Wynne once said that Hitler, as well as all his other crimes, was responsible for thousands of grazed knees.)

Another player in our story appears that night. Sid Curtis and the other members of the part-time band in the restaurant played on, but the replacement drummer was a pretty poor imitation of Sid's younger brother Harry. It was a pity that the two

Curtis brothers could not get leave at the same time. But Harry was spud bashing—locked up for the weekend by his superiors with a punitive mound of potatoes to be peeled for the cookhouse—a legacy from his recent activities associated with the black market and the sudden appearance of fresh eggs at RAF Swingate. So Sid was the only aircraftsman on stage that night. And he, coincidentally, had also worked for the post office before the war. Perhaps he noticed Mickey leaving the restaurant, although they hadn't yet met. But then the restaurant would have been filled with young servicemen like himself, soon to be sent overseas, wooing their girls with a kind of desperate gaiety. As for Sid—his sandy hair brilliantined, his saxophone gleaming, his lanky legs tapping to the beat—no doubt he cast his infectious grin at the likely girls, but he kept his heart intact as always—what was the point of starting something you might never be able to carry on?

Outside on the street there must have been

many young couples like Wynne and Mickey, clinging to each other under umbrellas, shivering on their way to the Tube station, lingering on corners to kiss each other through the scratchy wet wool of their scarves, until the wail of the air-raid siren sent them running for the shelter of the Underground's Central Line.

Preston Rd
Leytonstone

December 10th 1941

Dearest Darling,
First I want to tell you what a perfect weekend it's
been. Did you ever imagine that two people could be
so happy? Mickey, I'm so glad that we've always
known how lucky we are. Not like some people, who
don't even know what they've got until it's gone.
It was so good to be together and to go out on the
town again—I didn't even mind being caught in the
bombing! All that noise and chaos—the street rising
and falling, the blast pulling and pushing us—
I thought my eyeballs would be sucked out! But
I couldn't be frightened because you were there. And
then it was dawn, and we looked at each other and
saw we were black from head to foot—I've never
laughed so much—it was like having a coalman for

a husband! How I had to scrub to get you clean before you could go back to the station!

How could I let you go away without knowing where you are going? But I smiled and waved like you wanted—were you proud of me? I thought Scotland was far enough away—and soon you'll be overseas. What point is there in Christmas without you—I think they should banish it! How shall I manage tonight?—I can still smell you on my skin, perhaps I won't wash—then I can breathe you in all night long. They should invent a way to bottle people's smell—someone would make a fortune! Our first night apart not knowing when we'll see each other again! Goodnight my love,

> Your devoted and adoring wife,
> Wynne
>
> xxxxxxxxxxxxxxxxxxxxxx

So Wynne waved Mickey goodbye at the railway station and went home to spend a subdued Christmas with her parents. She knew he had sailed away but his destination was a secret—letters had to be posted to the records office at RAF Gloucester and forwarded. Wynne discovered she had a talent for letter writing and every evening she comforted herself by forging a connection with Mickey via pen and paper. Presumably these early letters caught up with him at his ports of call, but she had to wait a few weeks for a reply. And then the first letter arrived from sunny Durban to brighten Wynne's January days.

1942

Durban, South Africa
9th Jan 1942

Dear Heart,
I have just arrived in town and this is to tell you
that I'm safe and well and wishing so much that
you were with me——I love you. You would love
this place darling, the temperature would just suit
you and I can imagine you walking about looking
in all the lovely shops, and making up your mind
where we would go in the evening. Everywhere is
beautifully clean and well planned. The various
styles and colours of the buildings remind me of
a fairy city, in fact I am taken back all the time
to those sugar towns of my picture book days,
and those dream places we both like so much to
see portrayed in colour at the pictures. Remember
'Over the Rainbow'?

Tell Mum and Dad I think of them but I have
not written to them because I know they will see

this. Give my love, darling, to everybody. I hope that you are all keeping fit.

Perhaps I will take you around the town now and point out everything to you. You are with me in my heart, now and always,

Your loving husband,
Mickey

Then began the game in earnest. Waiting for the postman.

It sounded like a game, a schoolyard game. Well, schoolyard games were deadly earnest in their way. For so many young women waiting at home, the long-awaited letter could transform the day. Was it better to stay at home in the morning to waylay the postman and know at once what kind of a day it would be? Or was it preferable to go out early and dawdle home, prolonging the anticipation, turning the hoped-for pages in your mind?

For Wynne the weeks went very slowly, with not enough to do and no letter to sweeten the monotony. Doreen was busy with her new baby, Vi was working in munitions. Daphne was bombed out—her husband was also overseas, and she was looking for a place for her and the kids. Wynne decided to let them the house in Preston Road, since Mickey's parents had invited her to live with them in Walthamstow. That meant she was still near her friends, fortunately, but time on her hands and a shortage of cash encouraged her to look for a job. It was exciting to think of doing your bit for the war effort—better than the endless knitting of socks. And plenty of new opportunities had arisen for women, even married women. Wynne toyed with the idea of being a bus conductress—she liked meeting people and the uniforms were quite smart. Mickey's Dad heard of an office job going in the City. But she couldn't type, at least not properly! He said they were short-staffed and couldn't afford to be fussy, so why not give it a go? A well turned out girl with enthusiasm could go a long way at a time like this.

And so Wynne found herself on the morning train along with the bowler hat brigade.

Office life with its jokes, its flirtations, its new routines and challenges provided enough distraction during the day. A serious wartime staff shortage meant a girl could advance surprisingly quickly through the ranks. But there were still the weekends to while away. The Rialto at Leytonstone had reopened after the first war scare, so there was the cinema, friends, playing the piano, reading and rereading the poetry Mickey had introduced her to. And every evening, the letter writing. From the moment Mickey sailed away Wynne had written to him every single day. The letters were a diary of her thoughts and emotions. They told of her daily occupation in war-torn London, of her love and longing, and of her hopes and fears.

The House of Brooks
Monday March 2nd 1942 10.30 p.m.
Letter 14

Dearest, darling husband,
This is me, your girlie, beginning her weekly
news-letter to the best husband in the world. Do
you realise it's twelve weeks since I last saw you?
Isn't it awful—I can't bear to think of it, it's
so terrible. I'll bet your ears were burning today,
dear, I was talking so much about you at the office.
I described you as . . . well let's just say they all
know you're the best boy in the world. (I don't
want you getting too bigheaded!) I'm going quite
well in the office—especially for someone with no
shorthand. Oh, but the boss dictates so fast and
I have to write in longhand so quickly—I have a
terrible time deciphering it afterwards; it's lucky
I have a good memory! I think it's ruining my
handwriting, though—the only thing I was ever
good at at school. Still, as long as you can

*understand it, my sweet—nobody else will ever
have to read it, will they?*

Tuesday 10 p.m.

*I had to type up a ten-page report today, and then,
groan, groan, I had to run off copies on that awful
stencil duplicator. We have our own private war
going on, the duplicator and me. I call it Adolf.
Sometimes Adolf thinks it's winning and I say,
'Hold on, matey, this is the girl who ran the big
dipper single-handedly when she was fifteen years
old—and she ain't beaten yet!' Then it throws a lot
of ink at me, but after a good wrestle I usually
come out on top! I'm very tired so I'll have to say
goodnight, now. I think it's all this early rising, it
wears me out. At the top I've drawn you a picture
of me 'snuggying' down to give you your half-past-
ten kiss. You are remembering, aren't you, darling
Mickey? our time—10.30 Greenwich Meantime.
I'll see you in my dreams.*

Wednesday 10.30 p.m.

*Your brother arrived home last night, my darling,
and we all gave him a hero's welcome. His leg is
very weak still, I hope he will be able to stay home
for a while—they say the merchant navy is the most
dangerous business of all to be in, but, of course,
I would never say so to your Mum. It's lovely to
see him, but oh, sometimes he reminds me so much
of you and it hurts so much! I rushed upstairs to
be ready for our goodnight kiss. Come home soon,
my love!*

Thursday 11 p.m. Pay Day

*What a horrible day it's been, though—it hasn't
stopped raining all day, but did it stop your wee
wifey from going to the pictures?—it did not!
I was late up this morning, though, and had to
rush my routine. I've got it down to a fine degree.
I wake at seven o' clock—and think of you for ten*

minutes! Get up and go downstairs, light fire, put
kettle on, take a cup of tea to your Mum and Dad,
get my breakfast ready. 7.40 I do my exercises to
the wireless, 7.50 sit down to breakfast, eight o'clock
get dressed and listen to the news, half-past eight—
leave the house. Not bad is it, for someone who hates
getting up early?

Anyway, after I left the office at Bow this
evening, I went to have a cup of tea at Lyons and
then to the Savoy. But I found I was too early for
the film, so I went to the library for half an
hour—and guess what I read—The University
News! Well—it was on the table in front of me,
and I've had enough of war news, it's so depressing!
All we hear about is Hitler's U-boats sinking our
ships and Japan's successes in Asia! The article
was about a bloke of fifty-seven who passed his
university entrance and is now going in for his Arts
exam. I wish I could do something like that, I'd
love to have a proper education. You know so much
about music and poetry and books—I do miss you

reading to me in the evenings. I do try and read on my own, but it's not the same without you.

Anyway, the film I saw was Bette Davis in The Little Foxes—it was very good though fearfully morbid. It made me feel quite queer, really. It was a psycological study (I know I've left an 'h' out somewhere) of a horrible type of family. They were strange to say the least. Still, they were American— I hope there aren't any English families like that!

Did I tell you I love you today? Well I do— and I wish I could hear from you—just a few lines would do. I rang the BBC forces programme today about my birthday message to you—I do so hope you hear it. I'll give you a special half-past-ten kiss on your birthday—and you—you make sure you give me an extra special one back!

Friday 10.40 p.m.

Sweetheart—guess what??? You are now hearing from a very important person in the Prudential

*Assurance Co! It was a scream today—my boss
said 'Take a letter to the General Manager and
inform him that Mrs Brooks is now the
Administrative Clerk of this office.' I was typing
away—and believe it or not, I didn't know how
to spell my own title, darling—and my boss
was standing right beside me! Fancy being made
something you can't spell, I think it's hilarious,
don't you? But haven't I made progress in a
fortnight? I'm going to snuggy down into bed with
you now and reread your letter from Durban.
That was written in January, darling, but nothing
since then and it's now March! I hope I won't have
to wait much longer, I look forward to your letters
so much. Never mind, I know I mustn't complain,
there are probably lots of letters held up somewhere!
Goodnight, God bless. (I almost signed 'Yours
Faithfully'!)*

Saturday 9.30 p.m.

Hello Darling,
I haven't been in long—I've been walking under the
stars—not alone—ooh he was lovely! No, I can't
pretend, 'he' was Zoe's dog, Pat. Remember Zoe
from next door? She and I walked as far as the
waterworks. It's enjoyable out but still cold, and,
of course, when I look at the stars I can only think
of you and find it hard to carry on a conversation.
It seems to have been cold forever, I hope it's
warm where you are my sweet, wherever that is!
When I finished work today (at lunchtime, being
Saturday), I caught the bus to Leytonstone to see
Daphne, our tenant, and collect two weeks' rent.
Her sister, Jean, wants to come and live there with
her; Jean has a daughter, so that means three kids in
the house, but I said I didn't mind as long as they
look after the furniture. Who knows, maybe one
day we'll be lucky enough to have our own little
ones in that house—I can just picture you, my

sweet, reading to our children at bedtime! Shall we have boys or girls? I bet you'll spoil the girls! The house looked so lovely and cosy—how I wish we were there together now. But your Mum and Dad are very good to me, of course, so you mustn't worry about me.

I've been waiting for Vera Lynn's programme—I always hope you might be listening, too. She says her programme is a sort of rendezvous for husbands and wives who are separated. If you really were listening, sweet, how wonderful it would be! I usually sing along with her with tears in my eyes, and even bigger ones in my heart. I hope tonight she sings 'Yours'—that's what I am—yours. It conjures up such memories of you and I sitting hand in hand by the fire. Oh, Mickey, I just wish and pray for the day we'll be doing that again—I hate this business that keeps us apart—I hate it so much! I don't care about a 'free world'—I just want you home—the old affectionate you. You won't change will you? I can't bear to think of you

*changing. I'm sorry, I'm a bit depressed tonight.
Please God, let me have a letter!*

Sunday 9 p.m.

*We had to go down the shelter last night—quite a
surprise to hear the siren, other cities seem to cop it
these days, poor things. Remember in the Blitz when
we sat down there with you reading me poetry and
me knitting for the war effort? I swear I looked like
a bloody sock I knitted so many! And when we went
back indoors the woodwork on the windows was so
hot we couldn't touch it. It seemed like bad times
but at least you were with me and I'd give anything
to have that now. Anyway, I hope it stays quiet
tonight to finish the 13th letter. Darling, I have
written every night since I said goodbye to you—
86 days! 86 days is a lifetime, darling, isn't it?
I can't bear to think of it. I've also worked it out
in hours but I won't put that down in figures—it's
too upsetting. Back to the office, tomorrow—I'm*

1 Mickey and Wynne, 1940.

2 *Mickey's first letter from overseas, 9 January 1942.*

3 Harold (Mickey) Brooks.

I saw today,
The first ~~crocus~~ golden crocus,
Pushing its head, out of the
              cold earth,
Like a beam of ~~sunshine~~.
It had a message,
Full of hope,
Spring is on its way.

And now I know,
This cold winter around my
                        heart
Must surely pass,
As seasons do.
My spring must come
And with it dear
Fulfilment of my hopes and
                        dreams
Which really means
              Just You. "

4 Wynne's poem for Mickey's birthday, 18 March 1943.

getting quite an old hand at the insurance business.
You'd better be careful, darling, or the first thing
I shall be doing when I see you is selling you war
savings bonds! When I see you—doesn't that sound
good? I dream of it so much that the ecstasy of
seeing you would probably make me pass right out!
Better have some smelling salts ready. When I see
you—I like writing that, it makes it seem sort of
a near thing, which I think it will be, my dearest.
I'm going to bed to dream of it right now—dream
with me.

Your ever-loving
Wynne
xxxxxooooxxxxxooooxxxxx

And then the joy of a letter from on board ship, sent via Bombay—written on January 25th 1942 and not received until two months later.

Monday March 23rd 1942
Letter 17

My VERY dearest Mickey,
It's so wonderful to see your handwriting,
darling —oh thank you so much for this letter!
It does seem a long time since you wrote it—it's
dated 25th January—two months ago! Never mind,
it came, I don't think I could have managed another
day longer! I'm so pleased with it, sweetheart,
it's such a typical letter from my boy. The only
disappointing thing is I was hoping to see your
address on it and to know where you are stationed,
but I suppose I shall know soon. Your Mum and
Dad are as excited as I am and everyone sends
their love. I had been feeling so miserable since your
birthday last week—it's so hard not to know what
you are doing when I used to know every minute of
your day, and I wondered if you were celebrating,
or even if you remembered! (My brother, John, says
it's difficult to keep track of the date when you're in

action. *Are you at the battlefront now? Please God you keep safe for me—I want you to be careful, we have so much loving yet to do.) If you are still writing in your diary, as you promised, you would certainly have remembered—I put an extra special message on that page, didn't I? I hope you keep with your writing, I'm sure you'll be a famous author one day. I shall go to bed now and think of you on deck, thinking of me! I'm so sorry you've been seasick, but at least you won't want to go sailing off around the world when the war is over—I'm going to keep you here with me.*

> *God bless you my only love,*
> *Your Wynne*
> *xxxxxooooxxxxooooxxxx*
> *(hundreds of times!)*

PS Just imagine, while we were shivering in the snow, you were sunbathing on deck!

January 25th 1942

My Angel,
I feel as though I've been at sea for years, not
weeks. There was a time when I was always glad to
get to the seaside at every opportunity, but right now
I'd swap all the salt water in the world for a seat
under the lilac tree with you, my love.

When you married a civil servant you never
expected him to become a kitchen hand, did you?
But that's what my duties are on board—washing
meat tins and galley utensils! Do you know what
all this slopping about in dirty water and
wallowing in grease reminds me of? Being a child
and fishing in the drains—only now I'm not
punished for it! When I'm up on deck in the fresh
air and sunshine I think only of you and how
wonderful my life has been since I met you—even
though we now have to be apart.

Dear Heart, if ever I fell in love a second time,
it would be because I was falling in love with you

all over again. I could never have lost my heart to anyone else, it was yours from the start. If I had to begin my life all over, I'd still fall in love with you.

Goodnight Sweetheart,
Whatever happens, I'm always
with you.

What kind of life is a young man expecting when he marches off to war? A young man whose interests are poetry and music, who works behind a desk, and on weekends drives his pretty wife into the domesticated south-eastern English countryside in a Hillman Minx?

Presumably he expects parade grounds and the comfortless conviviality of the barracks. Perhaps, with excitement and dread in unequal measures, he anticipates the stench of blood and fear and cordite, the roar of the guns.

But what does a young man from Essex know of the Far East in the age before telecommunications, other than the stamps passed across his counter, or the Hollywood version of a Chu Chin Chow? Does he ever imagine the stagnation and barbarousness of a life behind barbed wire?

On February 15th 1942 Singapore fell, its defences facing the wrong way. The invaders came by bicycle, across the Malayan peninsula, while the forces of the Empire looked confidently seaward.

By the time Wynne received her treasured letter, Mickey had known for two weeks what it was like to be a prisoner of the Japanese.

Spirits were reasonably high to begin with among the POWs in Surabaya, Java. How to occupy your time, how to find a place to be alone—Sid said later that these were major considerations in the early days of the camp. Sid and Mickey weren't yet the close friends they became later under more exacting circumstances, but anyone who knew Mickey in the camps knew of his need for moments of solitary contemplation. One of his great gifts to his wife had been his ability to communicate on paper, to express thoughts and feelings he was too reticent to put into words. Now he was to be denied this solace, and Wynne was to be denied this legacy. According to Sid, Mickey's treasured diary was confiscated by the Japanese; the symbols for hugs and kisses inscribed by Wynne on every page misconstrued by his captors as a method of code. It was the genial and not normally reflective Sid who recalled for us later the picture of Mickey sitting in the evenings and 'writing to Wynne in his mind'. It was Sid who described, reluctantly, the conditions in the camps.

From the first, the scarcity and repetitive nature of the food—a little rice boiled in a great deal of water until it took on the consistency of glue, sometimes beans and a few vegetables—left the prisoners weak and faint.

Once they were given a carcass by the guards—they thought it must be a pig—but it was so rotten they could not risk eating it. Grasshoppers and rats were valuable sources of nutrition. Sid couldn't remember how they tasted—they never touched the sides as they went down!

Early games of football soon had to cease in order to conserve strength, and anyway, as Sid recalled, there were arguments with the Australians over the merits of the different rules. (They kept running away with the ball!) Indeed arguments were a part of daily life; tempers flared as men in dreadfully crowded conditions sought to preserve their own allotted space. Mickey envied those with practical skills who could find ways of making themselves, and others, comfortable. The intellectual and artistic abilities admired in the life the prisoners came from suddenly seemed to command less respect. In the world of the camp very different talents made men most in demand. Those who earned status were the ones who could build themselves a nest from the camp's detritus, scrounge extra food, bargain with the villagers they met while on work parties and thereby smuggle a small luxury back into the camp, in a boot or under a hat. These seemed to be the skills for survival. However, there were also opportunities for camaraderie. Small discussion groups strove to exercise their minds, and here Mickey and Sid became friends by inventing their own Brains Trust—with language rather more colourful than the BBC!

Wynne's great burden, meanwhile, was the lack

of news. No letter, no means of knowing Mickey's whereabouts. Still she wrote, every day. Once a week she posted the letters to the India Command, praying that somehow they were getting through and helping to raise his morale in whichever hellish theatre of war he was facing.

Monday April 13th 1942
Letter 20

My Mickey,
Three weeks now since your last, January letter
arrived. Every day and still no word from you, the
disappointment makes me quite sick. I've written
again to RAF Records Gloucester, perhaps they'll
reply this time. If only I had some idea where you
are it would be easier, but the world is such a big
place and you may be in any part of it. Oh,
darling heart, where are you? It never occurred to
me I would have to wait four months not knowing
your whereabouts. I'm so lonely without you,
I shall never get used to it. I always wear the watch
you gave me, it's keeping splendid time, everyone in
the office sets theirs by it. I've been listening to the
Budget news. Beer is going up twopence a pint!
And the pictures are going up from ninepence to a
shilling. Not that I go much any more. Remember
how I loved the pictures? I just hate going places

alone. Really, I think if I had known what I was to go through I would have done you an injury or something, anything to keep you at home! Your brother says one day I'll come home and I won't be able to open the front door, there'll be such a crowd of letters on the mat. Just one would do me for going on with. Blimey, I do sound sorry for myself, don't I? I just miss you so terribly and worry about you so much. I know how you must be hating war, it doesn't suit your nature at all. How shall we spend your first days home when all this is over? I can imagine you chuckling—alright, I know we will be easily occupied! I suppose, though, I shall have to share you with the family—I mean, they'll want to spend time with you. Do you think when that blessed day comes I would be able to keep your homecoming secret for a couple of days? No, of course I wouldn't, I'll be shouting it from the rooftops! I feel like shouting now—all the way across the sea to wherever you are. 'COME HOME!'

Tuesday 10.30 p.m.

COME HOME! COME HOME!

You see, I'm still shouting inside my head.
Someone at work today said I looked so fierce—it
must have been all that concentration! How are you,
my love? I hope you're eating properly. I wonder if
you have the sort of rationing we have here. I'm so
sick of carrots, they're in every recipe in every
magazine, from soup to pudding. See in the dark?
We'll be able to see from here to Timbuctoo. Perhaps
I should eat some more and then I could see you,
wherever you are! I write such nonsense, I hope you
don't get bored by it. Perhaps I should go to bed
(I shan't need a light—I'll be able to see in the
dark!).

Wednesday 9 p.m.

SEND HIM HOME! SEND HIM HOME!

I think, dearest, I'm shouting to the wrong

person when I shout in my head at you. You're too conscientious to run away, even if it were possible. No, I shall have to shout at your commanding officers, and if I keep on it might get through, somehow. I'm so tired at the moment because I'm having to work late, everyone in the office seems to be going down with a cold, and yours truly is always so healthy she soldiers on and does her bit regardless! So it's early bed all this week. (More time to dream of you!)

Thursday 9 p.m.

SEND HIM HOME! SEND HIM HOME! (still shouting)

Friday 9 p.m.

SEND HIM HOME! SEND HIM HOME!

Saturday 10 p.m.

*I was 'digging for victory' with your Dad today.
We're turning the flowerbed under the peach tree
into yet another vegetable patch. Oh no, more
carrots! I think I have blisters coming on my
hands—I hope not, it's back to the typewriter on
Monday. I've stopped shouting. Vi reminded me
that if you were sent home unexpectedly it would
probably be because you were wounded. Of course
I don't want any harm to come to you, my love.
I must trust in Fate. If Fate is a woman like in
poetry, then she'll know how I'm feeling and
she'll keep you safe and send you home when she's
ready. Now I'm going to whisper instead—listen
carefully!*

   I LOVE YOU!

       Your lonely wifey
       Wynne

Monday 21st April
Letter 21

My Own Dear Love,
I've been over to Wanstead, did you enjoy our walk
in the forest? I chatted to you all the way—the
weather is beautiful and it's so hard you're not here
to share this lovely Spring with me. I pointed out
the leaves on the lime trees to you—all bursting
through after their winter slumber, and so curly
and sweet. I worked in our garden—the lilac's
out already, it's going to be wonderful this year.
Oh, and guess what your girlie did—I mended
a fuse, see how competent I'm getting? Perhaps
I could go to evening classes in carpentry or
something and really surprise you. The trouble is
I don't like going out at night any more, especially
in the blackout. Not like the old me, is it? Now,
instead of dancing the night away, my favourite
occupation is to go to bed and think of you. I did
have another favourite occupation in bed if you

remember, but for that I need you to assist me!

I have some new undies, all silky. Well, you have to buy when you see them—they may not be in the shops next week. I'm saving them for when you come home. They're called 'Glamorous Seduction'. Now the weather is getting warmer we girls will be able to go bare legged—you just can't get decent stockings. You'd laugh if you could see me, I paint my legs with gravy browning and then your Dad paints the seam with my eyebrow pencil. He says it's his 'war work'! It looks very authentic until it rains, then we have legs like streaky bacon! It's a bit different to when I was modelling at Liberty's and we thought we were so chic. The first time I used a cigarette holder I did an elegant turn and burnt a hole in the next girl's fur coat! I don't bother with smoking any more, cigarettes are getting more and more difficult to come by.

Dearest love, you owe me 3,546 kisses—that's a meagre one an hour. You are going to be very busy when you get home . . .

1942

Wednesday 23rd April

*A reply from the Air Ministry at last, after I'd
made all sorts of enquiries about you by wire, letter
and telephone. But what a reply! Nothing but
a carefully worded, stencilled letter that told me
nothing at all. My heart tells me you're safe and
my heart can't be wrong; but my head imagines
all kinds of things and I think I'll go crazy! What
upsets me the most is that the Air Ministry don't
even know where you are. I'm to write to the
Records Office at Gloucester and not to India
Command. Oh sweetheart, this isn't fair! I've been
writing and writing every day and imagined you
receiving my letters, and now I don't know if any
of them ever reached you, and from now on will
they even leave the country? It's so hard, I never
knew it would be this hard. Your Dad says they
can't tell me where you are because it's probably
top secret, and that's why you haven't been able to*

write ... *It does make me feel a little bit better, but I really hate this War, it all seems so bloody stupid!*

I like what you said once, that this separation is like too long an interval in a play about two very happy people. We are truly happy, aren't we darling? Nothing can really separate us.

> *I love you, love you, love you,*
> *Wynne*
>
> xxxxooooxxxxooooxxxx

May 4th 1942
Letter 23

Dearest Darling,
You'll see from the number at the top that this is
the 23rd letter. I wonder how many you've received.
It's my holidays just now and I've been up to
Alexandra Palace. The cherry blossoms are just
wonderful. I sat under them and thought of you.
I remembered feeding you cherries—I'd loop them
over my ear like earrings and you'd bite them off!
While I was sitting there someone passed by in
uniform and for a moment he looked so like you.
Then he turned, and I saw he wasn't really like you
at all. The Yanks are everywhere, suddenly. They're
great fun, but goodness they can be cheeky sods!
John reckons there will be a big push into North
Africa soon. That brother of mine got himself into
a fight with a Yank over a taxi. I must say they do
all seem to be appropriated by the Americans. Still
no letter from you, it's so strange. Where are you at

this moment, what are you doing? The little boy
next door taught me a song:

> *Whistle while you work,*
> *Hitler is a twerp,*
> *Goering's barmy, so's his army,*
> *Whistle while you work.*

I sang it at the Ferry Boat last night when we went
to celebrate Stan and Vi's engagement. Vi's Mum had
made a cake. At least she said it was a cake—it
looked like one, and I know she had to beg, borrow
and steal to get the sugar, but, honestly it tasted
more like sawdust and glue! Vi's sister, Marge, has
an American boyfriend and he was showing us
how to jitterbug, it was a scream. And guess what
happened to Marge, I would have died if it had
happened to me! You just can't get elastic at the
moment because of the fall of Singapore and no
rubber industry, and this new celanese material is
so slippery the buttons come undone. So Marge is

dancing away when HER KNICKERS FELL DOWN!
Well, you can imagine, we just couldn't stop
laughing. I'd have been so embarrassed, but you
know Marge, bold as brass, she picks them up
without breaking her step and waves them like a
flag as she dances off to the ladies! It was good to
have a laugh.

Then we drank to your health, my sweet,
although the ache around my heart was unbearable.
Still no letter from you. I hope, wherever you are,
that my letters are helping you to keep your chin
up. Don't you go looking at any exotic foreign
girls now! You just remember that you're mine,
sweetheart.

May 6th

My darling,
Sometimes I think I can hardly bear it. I wake up
in the morning and I remember. I get this awful
lump in my throat when I think of another day
to be spent without you. When I passed Gertie's
yesterday, she came dashing out with a letter from
her husband, AND some snapshots! I tried to be
pleased for her, I really did. I thought, surely
there'll be something from my darling, and I ran all
the way home, but there wasn't. All this waiting—
I'm so miserable my love. But I try to carry on,
I try to be your brave, laughing girl, I know I have
to keep well for when you come home.

I'm enclosing a picture of a bluebell wood. Isn't
it just like the one we saw near Hastings? We'll be
there again my love, I know we will.

Your everloving
Wynne

On Haroekoe Island, in the Molucca Archipelago, Sid and Mickey were put to work building an airstrip for the Japanese forces, which the prisoners hoped would be bombed by the Allies, despite the danger to themselves. The journey by sea had been a nightmare: seventeen days aboard the *Amagi Maru*, hundreds of men battened down in the hold in tropical heat, with no water and the constant fear of being torpedoed and sent to the bottom by your own side. Most of the prisoners had sold their few possessions for extra food. Few had mosquito nets and there were no medical supplies to treat their rapidly deteriorating health. The flimsy bamboo structures, which could hardly be termed huts and were no protection form the rain, were built alongside open, overflowing latrine trenches.

By June 1942 both Sid and Mickey were suffering from amoebic dysentery, malaria and beri-beri. Here a blanket could save your life, and the two men looked out for one another and by putting the other's needs first, managed to create a small family unit. Within the camp it became vitally important not to stand on your own—to have someone else to care for. Sid stated often that it was the youngest men who died first, those with perhaps no overview of life, no dependants at home, little spiritual reserve in the face of brutality. As the men cut rocks at the bottom of a quarry, the guards, some of them released from Japanese gaols, threw more rocks down at them. The cuts from these developed into ulcers that refused to heal.

When a very young prisoner fell over the edge of the quarry, they tipped a skip of rocks on top of him and buried him, without waiting to see if he was still alive. Men were beaten for the slightest 'offence'. One day for smiling, another day for not smiling.

There was no way to anticipate the cruelty of officers like 'Bamboo' Mori. To Sid and Mickey he was beyond comprehension—an aesthete, with a Japanese love of beauty and harmonious spareness, yet so christened by the prisoners because a few cuts from his cane could leave you badly scarred or even dead. For some of the prisoners the constant fear and uncertainty engendered hopelessness, and soon their vacant expressions marked them for an early demise.

And still Wynne wrote. She told him always of her longing but otherwise strove to entertain. War news was gloomy and much of it wouldn't have passed the censor anyway. She spared him the dark events of her life—her brother John wounded, Doreen's Stan killed at El Alamein. She didn't mention the Lancaster bomber crew on leave whom the girls in her office all entertained in the pub one evening, only to find out a week later that on the crew's next mission they all went out, high-spirited as usual, and not one of them came back.

15th June
Letter 29

My Own Love,
Are you reading my daily message in your diary?
When I wrote 'I love you' on every one of the 365
days I never dreamt we'd be apart for so much of
it. Do you remember how worried I was when you
first joined up that you'd be posted somewhere in
England where I couldn't stay near you? I couldn't
bear to be separated from you for even a few hours.
Do you think I was greedy? Was I wrong to want
you so much? This is truly more terrible than
anything I could have imagined, but I know you
must be alright or my heart would tell me
differently. Hilda heard from Jimmy in Lahore
and he said he was separated from you at Durban.
They went to Ceylon, but he seems to think your
unit was bound eventually for Singapore. Your
Mum and Dad and I have been poring over maps
and we feel that after you left Bombay you couldn't

have reached Singapore before it fell, could you?
No, you must be safe! Imagine me who never
knew where Singapore was. Now I know so much
about geography I could have been a navigator on
your ship!

Darling one, six centuries couldn't be as long as
this six months. I've had to organise a new tenant
for our house. We've lost Daphne, and good riddance
to bad rubbish! Can you believe she was carrying on
with another man and now she's gone to live with
him, and her husband overseas! When I arrived
there was a letter on the mat from the poor man.
I felt quite sick! Anyway, we shall soon be living
there again, I hope, as cosy as can be.

My darling I was going through your things
today and I found the manuscript of the book you
were writing. I can't wait for you to come home
and finish it so that I can be married to a famous
author! Then we can have a cottage in the country
and you can smoke a pipe and I can have a swing
in the apple tree. I aired your clothes in the garden,

and I kissed your suits and imagined you wearing them. And I found the blue satin nightie I put away after our honeymoon. I'm saving it for our next honeymoon when you return—it can't be long now!

I've had a new suit made—I used practically a year's clothing coupons! It took me ages to find the cloth. Your Mum thinks it's too flashy, but why do we have to wear gloomy clothes all the time just because there's a war on? You have to keep your chin up! Your Mum and I went to a meeting at the Spiritualist Church at Walthamstow. Edith at the butchers told Mum about it so we thought we'd give it a go. I wasn't sure if you'd approve, but really, darling, they're awfully nice people. I don't know what to think of it all really. The medium picked me out several times during the service and said she had messages from the spirit world through her Red Indian guide! The spirits said I must stop thinking dark thoughts, and that I had healing powers if I learnt how to use them! It was a bit embarrassing really but I talked to her afterwards and she said that you and I have such a strong bond of love that we can never really be separated. Of course we know that anyway, don't we? She also said I must only think loving, happy thoughts because my thoughts reach you and good thoughts will help keep you safe. She reminded me of you in a way—you believe so much in people and in being optimistic about the future. Remember how you always said we're fighting for a better world and good would come of it all? I'm really going to try to be positive. And I think I'll go to the Spiritualist Church again—it's quite comforting really.

> I love you,
> Your wife and sweetheart,
> Wynne xxxxxx
> xxxxxx

20th July 1942
Letter 34

Hello Sweetheart,
I went to help your Dad this evening at the
allotment. I don't have any overalls so I wore my
old jodhpurs, and a scarf over my hair. I said,
'Are you requiring a land girl?' He didn't recognise
me at first, then he kept making horsey type jokes—
that I was galloping over his lettuces, and to take
the bit between my teeth and dig in my hooves and
so on. It was funny to begin with but I think my
laugh was a bit forced after a while! Poor Dad, he
thinks it's his duty to cheer me up and stop me
worrying. Actually we all try and keep cheerful for
each other but it's a relief sometimes to have a little
cry on my own in my room. I wonder if they do
the same—I hope not.

Darling Heart I love you and miss you so, but
I'm trying to think and plan only for the time when
you will be with me again. The medium at the

Spiritualist Church picked on me again and told me not to worry—the spirits say if I worry it casts such a dark condition over my loved ones. I want to be helpful and make things better for you, not worse, so I am trying to think only happy thoughts.

I went with Vi to a dance at the Fire Station— all the fire engines were put out the back, and of course a few couples went missing and were later found smooching and goodness knows what else in the cabs and even on top of the engines! We taught some Canadians how to do Knees Up Mother Brown! It was a laugh, I did feel quite cheered up, although some of the Canadians got very drunk, and we left quite early and had a cocoa at Vi's. You stick to cocoa now, won't you? I've just realised I've never seen you drunk, although I wouldn't really blame you if you went on a bender now and then, you must need to let your hair down and drown your sorrows and all that. This bad dream will all be over one day and there will be no more sorrows.

24th August 1942
Letter 39

Darling Husband of Mine,
Florence came over after tea while I was pressing
some frocks and we decided to go over to see my
mum. I hadn't seen her for a couple of weeks
and she looked very well. She was wearing a new
costume and a white blouse, and she's bought a new
hat too. It was the nicest I've seen her look for ages,
I do think the work she's doing with the Red Cross
is suiting her. It's only making up parcels, but it
gets her out of the house. I teased her by saying
I'll bet she puts messages in the parcels for the boys
overseas. Vi says they do that in munitions. Have
you ever had a message from a girl back home? If
you do and there's an address to write to I want
to know about it! If only you could write home,
or are your letters lost somewhere? My darling the
lack of news is so hard to bear, how can I not be
worried, whatever the spirits say? The medium said

last week that she had a message to convey to me but it was only to 'keep my chin up'. She didn't say it was from the spirits so I wondered if it was your thoughts passed on by a vibration of some sort. We believe, don't we, that thoughts can be telegraphed between people—maybe she has the power of receiving them. Oh, it's 10.30 p.m.—time for our kiss! What wouldn't I give for a real one. My goodness, this is awful, we shall forget how to kiss, but I don't propose you practise on any of the lads. I think we'll soon pick up where we left off!

Don't forget, dear, that in reality I am always by your side,

xxxxxxxxxxxxxxxxxxx
x Your Devoted &
Adoring Wife, x
x Wynne x

xxxxxxxxxxxxxxxxxxx

September 14th 1942
Letter 42

My Own Love,

I played the piano this evening, very softly, and you sang to me just as you used to. Do you know what you sang? 'Always'. Remember all the times you sang that to me, sweetheart? I am always remembering—that's all I have to live on, memories and future dreams coming true.

Your sisters came today with the children so there was such a clatter round the teatable! And goodness, Nellie can talk, can't she? Little Terry and Eddie were very glum because your Dad had told them because he was so sick of meat rationing he was going to have their pet rabbit for Sunday lunch! I told them he was only joking and that their old rabbit was probably far too tough to make a good meal. They cheered up then and we played dominoes. I think your sister Eva likes me better than she used to. When they'd gone I had a bath and washed my hair, in the obligatory five inches of water, of course. I've forgotten how it feels not to have to save on fuel, and I've become an expert at washing up with half a kettle of water. It's the winter I dread, of course. We keep the sitting room warm but the upstairs is absolutely freezing. With the evenings drawing in we're all reminded of how miserable a wartime winter is. God grant it all ends soon. I've quite a bit of paper left and no more news to tell you so I'll fill it with the most important words of all.

I LOVE YOU

I LOVE YOU

I LOVE YOU

Take care of yourself, best and dearest husband, and remember wherever you are I am always by your side. I wonder if you talk to me as I do to you,

and if you hear me answer as I hear you?
Goodnight my dearest, God Bless You and protect
you and keep you safe for your

D. & A. L. Wife xxxxxxxxxxxx
Wynne xxxxxxxxxxxxxx

In October some news filtered through, but such news as would bring a new burden of worry. The likelihood that Mickey was a prisoner could no longer be denied.

October 12th 1942

My Dearest Dear
Hilda has had another letter from Jimmy in
India. He's heard you were last seen in Java.
I'm beginning to think you must still be there,
that you must be a prisoner. Oh my angel, what if
you're ill or hurt somewhere and I can't be with
you, can't help you? I feel as though my heart is
swollen with the pain, that it will burst out of my
body and leave me empty. Hilda says I must send
only a one-page letter once a week to Tokyo, typed
so they can read it easily. She says a short letter has
much more chance of getting through. It was a small
enough pleasure, my nightly letters to you, but it
seems I'm not even to have that comfort now.

> *I pray for you, my love, day and night*
> *Your own*
> *Wynne*

Sid and Mickey spent much of their little spare time endeavouring to keep their clothes mended and their bodies clean, but as many of the work-force sickened and died the remainder were forced to work seven days a week, and often late into the night. Tenko was another form of hell. For the slightest misdemeanour the guards would turn roll call into an endurance test. Standing in the sun for hours without hat and shirt (exchanged for extra rations to build up Mickey's strength after a bad bout of dengue fever), Sid's fair skin smouldered, and germinated the cancers that were to plague him later. Shoulder to the wheel, ordered to rescue a Japanese cart, Mickey lost his boots in the mud. Sid joked that soon his boots would be big enough for both of them. So thin and stooped, skin purple from beri-beri, he nicknamed them both the Shrinking Violets.

At night Mickey struggled to remember favourite lines of poetry, but the lively discussions of the early days disappeared as the apathy of the camp overtook them, and the world outside receded.

Wynne, meanwhile, continued to follow Hilda's advice and despatched her short, formal letters in the hope that they would reach Tokyo and ultimately the camp. It must have felt suddenly like writing to a stranger, and when, just before Christmas, some letters were returned, she gladly reverted to her emotional, newsy letters sent via the Records Office.

Sunday 20th December 1942

Another Christmas to face without you, how can I celebrate? I wish I could hibernate over the holiday season. I smile only with my lips, my heart is waiting for you before it smiles again. I no longer write to Tokyo—my letters were returned. I'm back to writing to Gloucester Records Office. If only I knew you had received some of my letters as a Christmas present I should be so happy, and just a line from you would make such a difference to my spirits. Remember our favourite Rachmaninov record that got broken in the Blitz? Well I bought us a new one for Christmas and I play it all the time and imagine us sitting by the fire, hand in hand, and all the ugly grey world locked outside.

I'm chief clerk now and in charge of the office at Bow, so it was up to me to organise the Christmas party, although I must confess I have never felt less like partying, my sweet. We had quite a good tea for wartime and a tree decorated with coloured paper.

And we played forfeits and I had to do a dance so
I pretended to be Shirley Temple and sang 'On the
Good Ship Lollipop', it was a scream! Mr Forrest,
one of the reps, reckons I'm on my way to
Hollywood, but I said I needed some curls to be
another Shirley Temple and I don't like myself
with curls so I don't think I'll go to Hollywood.
I think I'll go on being Mrs Brooks and stay here
and wait for you!

All this forced gaiety feels so hollow. Christmas
is about peace—and we have none. And about
love—well at least we know what that is, you and
I. If only everyone could love just one other person
as much as we love one another, then surely there'd
be no wars—because when you really love nothing
else matters.

Goodnight Dear One
Your loving Wynne

xxxxxxxxx

On Christmas Day 1942, Mickey and the other prisoners were allowed to sign official postcards and address them to their loved ones. The messages claimed they were well treated, but despite their indignation, the men had no wish for those at home to know the truth. No mail was delivered to the prisoners. The frustration of not knowing how the war was going was compounded by the ridiculous propaganda fed to them by the Japanese. (Japanese navy heroes kept ships from colliding by holding them apart; Britain would soon surrender because of starvation caused by failure of their rice crop!)

Sid was Mickey's lifeline. Sid could find a joke in most things, and his lively disposition reminded Mickey of Wynne. Through the nights of sweat and mud and jungle noises, Mickey would recall for Sid walks with Wynne under frosty stars, Wynne under the lilacs in their spring garden—how he hated to miss the spring—the scent of her hair, her gaiety on the dance floor. The hope of holding her again kept him alive. She was, he said, his secret weapon.

Though she found it more and more difficult to believe Mickey was receiving her letters, Wynne continued to write—it was the only connection between them. On good days she was certain he felt the power of her love emanating like waves across the planet. On bad days she fought to recall his face, his voice. His smell lingered less and less on his clothes.

1943

January 2nd 1943

My Darling

A new year, and surely it will see us reunited?
I made it my New Year's wish, so fervently that
I don't think our guardian angels would dare ignore
it! It's cold and frosty here and everything is all
silvery and sparkly in the moonlight, just as you
love it. Wartime spoils everything, though; we
always thought moonlight so romantic but now a
full moon, a 'bomber's moon' is bad news—just an
invitation to Jerry.

Dearest I do not write every single day as I used
to, but not because I think of you any less, believe
me you are in my heart and mind every minute of
the day. I know I promised to write every day and
I did for so long, it's just that until I hear from
you I cannot be sure you are receiving anything
from me and sometimes I feel all my writing is in
vain. If you are getting my letters, as I hope you

*are, I know you'll understand that I love you
and pray for you (and for us) just as much as
I ever did.*

*I have some sewing to do this evening although
I am not looking forward to it. My Mum managed
to get some flour bags which we bleached, and we're
turning them into sheets and teatowels for Florence's
wedding present. We just didn't appreciate the nice
things we had before the war, but I don't think I'll
ever take anything for granted again when it's over.
I don't like working with the flour bag material,
though. It doesn't have any 'give', if you see what
I mean. I'm sure Flo will be pleased, though. She's
going to have a white wedding in spite of all the
difficulties. Apparently she knows a woman who
can make a marvellous dress out of chemist's gauze,
and Aunty Edna is letting her have a couple of lace
tablecloths to cut up. (Actually they're more cream
than white but that will probably suit Flo better
with her red hair.) I've been thinking a great deal
about our own wedding, dearest; I didn't mind at*

all not wearing white, and our 'honeymoon' in our own little house couldn't have been any better if we'd been to the Riviera, in spite of the neighbours' teasing because the black-out never came down! Every moment I have shared with you couldn't be any more perfect and I know I am very lucky to have such lovely memories to keep me going until you come home again.

Be loved. I love you!
Wynne
xxxoooxxxoooxxx

February 14th 1943

Dear Heart,
That's how your letter would start if a letter had
come on this special day. I never give up hope but
my heart is very heavy as I write as there is still no
news of you, and particularly so because a woman
around the corner has had news of her son from
Java. I suppose, sweetheart mine, that there is no
reason for me to feel like this, but somehow I was
confident that yours would be one of the first names
to get through to me. It's silly, I know, and I have
been brave as I can be. Sorry sweetheart, I really
must 'dry up'. After all, my darling, it's so much
worse for you.

Mickey, you will always be my Valentine and
however long they keep us apart, that will never
change. When I'm with you, every day is like
Valentine's Day, and if Errol Flynn were to walk
into this room at this moment I wouldn't notice him
because the only image in my head is always of you.

(Actually your Dad walked in as I was writing that—in his dressing gown with a woolly hat on because it's so cold in the kitchen! He doesn't know why I am laughing so much!)

I'm glad today's over because it brings me nearer to tomorrow and the possibility of a letter from you.

> *Goodnight, my precious own truelove,*
> *from your loving Valentine*
> *xxxxxxxxxxxxxx*

March 18th 1943

*Today is a very special day, so I'm writing you
a very special letter. I lay in bed at 1 a.m. this
morning and wished you Many Happy Returns,
many, many of them, and all with me. I pretended
you were there and perhaps you were there,
sweetheart. How I ache for you! I want you to
touch me so much!*

*This is my birthday poem for you. I don't
suppose it's a very good poem—you know so much
about poetry. But I feel it's right for today, so I
hope you like it.*

> *I saw today
> The first golden crocus,
> Pushing its head out of the cold earth
> Like a beam of sunshine.
> It had a message, full of hope,
> That Spring is on its way.*

And now I know
This cold winter around my heart
Must surely pass as seasons do.
My Spring must come,
And with it dear, fulfilment of my hopes
    and dreams,
Which really means—
    Just you.

    From your adoring
    Wynne

May 5th 1943

My Darling One,

Oh, the lilacs, the lilacs! The one by the front gate is especially beautiful, like a purple cloud and smelling just like heaven (only not my heaven—you have to be with me for me to be in heaven). Sometimes they lift my heart so, I want to sing, and sometimes they make me feel the loss of your dear presence so keenly I feel I could weep tears of lead. I cannot imagine how I managed before I met you. Now I know that every experience is better when it's shared—shared with you, of course.

Now sweetheart, this is a famous actress talking to you—famous in Walthamstow, anyhow. I told you that I was going to be in Major Barbara at the Town Hall, well I played my first role last night to a packed house—people standing everywhere. Your Mum and my Mum were in the audience and were very proud, as I know you would have been. I don't suppose I would have been asked to do it if they

hadn't been so short of men, and naturally I would
have rather had a girl's role, but everyone said
I made a very good boy and Adolphus Cousins is
a very good part. I think it must be harder to act
a boy than a girl, anyway (when you're a girl,
I mean) so I think everyone was very pleased with
me and I was very pleased with myself! I think
people really like to see a play because so many of
the theatres in London are closed. So many of the
companies perform at the provincial theatres instead,
it's easier now to see good theatre in the country
than it is in town. I would love to go and see
Flarepath, though, about the wives of a bomber crew
waiting anxiously for their husbands to return.
(I know all about waiting, don't I?) It's written
by Terence Rattigan and Olive Barker says it's
very good and very popular.

   I hope you see me onstage one day, although
I won't want to be away from you for one minute
and rehearsals did take up a lot of evenings, so
perhaps I'll stay home instead! Olive did ask me if

*I want to be in the next one, but I told her I have
too much to do with work and helping your Mum
and my Mum, which is true. And writing to you,
of course. And dreaming about you, which takes up
more time than anything!*

From your leading lady,
Wynne

30th June 1943

Darling Mickey,

I think you must have found my letters (if you
have received them) very dull lately. It's been so
busy at work and I don't want to always be telling
you about people there that you don't even know.
I haven't had time to see many friends. Poor
Minnie had such a terrible time with her baby
and then it was stillborn. I've tried to spend some
time with her.

We have had some funny times, though. Florence
bought a homeperm (14s.6d.!) and I went over to
do it for her on Saturday. I read all the instructions
carefully and I think I did a good job. The curlers
were only bits of wire (you can't even buy hairgrips
because of the shortages) and very hard to put in,
but the real problem was the smell of the lotion—
poor Flo smelt like a manure heap! We had to sit in
the garden while it set but I still couldn't bear to be
near her. Her Mum had made some sandwiches and

we went through a performance of passing her the plate, and a cup of tea, on the end of the garden spade! It's a good job her new husband is away because apparently it still smells bad and she's taken to long walks in the fresh air, hoping the wind will blow the smell away! It is getting better, apparently, but meanwhile she's getting lots of exercise which can't be bad, she is a bit on the chubby side if you remember.

It must be strange for you, with so many new experiences and new faces in your life, to hear me talking of all the old people and places. Does my life seem very narrow to you? I hope it might be comforting when you're so far from home to know that things go on more or less the same, but I can't really tell. Sometimes everything I write about seems so trivial but I know you'll forgive me because you love me. You do still love me, don't you sweet? I can hear you answering 'very much' and I don't think it's wishful thinking. Anyway I remember how you used to like to hear me chatter

about the little (and big) things that happen to you.
I hope you wouldn't spare me the dangerous things
so as not to worry me. I want to be a part of
everything in your life, good and bad. We've had so
many good things and the bad part must be over
soon. Then there'll be nothing but good times, wait
and see—we deserve it, my love, after all this
waiting. They are playing, 'Ah, sweet mystery of life
at last I've found you' on the wireless. You are my
sweet mystery, the day I found you was the very
best day, but not as good as will be the day you
come home to me again.

Loving and praying for you,
Wynne xxxxxxxxxxxx

August 18th 1943

My Own Darling,
As you know, dearest, it was my birthday yesterday,
and up to the last moment I was praying for a
word from you, but it was not to be. We had tea in
the garden—it hasn't rained in ages and we used
the stirrup pump to water the beds. Everything looks
so dry and parched, which is how I feel—dry and
parched and empty without you, my love. I think
perhaps I can't write any more just now, everything
is so painful. Only know that I love you more than
anything.

Your Loving Birthday Girl
Wynne xxxxxxxxxxx

September 28th 1943

Dearest Mickey,

The war is going so much better for us now! We're winning in the Atlantic and it's surely only a matter of time with Japan (I don't care who reads this)—so just hang on, my love. Everywhere you go you realise people are more hopeful and so you can't help but feel glad, and I'm daring to hope that all will be well with you and I shall see you very soon.

I sat by the window doing needlework with your Mum this afternoon while she told me all the little incidents of your childhood, and we laughed to think of how we will spoil you when you come home. My Mum and Dad gave me a box of paints for my birthday last month. I'm tinting your photograph and I think I've got the colour of your eyes just right. Soon, please let it be soon, I will be able to see the real thing. Your eyes always have a smile

in them, did you know that? Keep smiling for me,
my love.

> God Bless You Always
> Your ever-loving Wynne

5 *Wynne Brooks.*

6 Top: *Mickey and Wynne, 1941.*
Bottom: *Returned letter, November 1945.*

Charges to per

POST OFFICE

No. OFFICE STAMP

REC * 81 E 17 77 361 12 1681 21 ST 1943 * A

Prefix. Time handed in. Office of Origin and Service instructions. Words.

31

m 5.32 LONDON CTO OHMS 65

From   To

PRIORITY CC V MRS H H BROOKS 81 HIGHAM HILL ROAD
                              WALTHAMSTOW E

FROM AIR MINISTRY 77 OXFORD ST W 1 REF OX 361 -
DEEPLY REGRET TO INFORM YOU THAT YOUR HUSBAND 1201681
AC 1 HAROLD HERBERT BROOKS IS REPORTED TO HAVE DIED
WHILST A PRISONER OF WAR IN JAPANESE HANDS ON 21 ST
OCTOBER 1943 THE AIR COUNCIL EXPRESS THEIR PROFOUND
SYMPATHY LETTER FOLLOWS SHORTLY - UNDER SECRETARY OF

7 *Telegram from Air Ministry, 29 November 1945.*

8 Wynne and Sidney Curtis, circa 1960.

Sid spent some time in the dreaded bamboo cage. Hot wires were pushed down his fingernails. During his torture the guards kept insisting he was Australian, presumably because of his height and fair hair; they were particularly severe with the Australians. It seemed for a while that Mickey would have to continue alone, but Sid survived. They told each other that the war couldn't last forever and as they'd endured so much already it wasn't unrealistic, they assured each other, to hope for a good outcome; but, just in case, if only one survived he would visit the other's family when the madness was over. Sid promised he would deliver Mickey's watch, a gift from his wife, but surveying his own legs and feet, bloated and purple from beri-beri, he privately feared it would be his own mother weeping on the doorstep as a stranger recounted her son's death.

In October 1943 the Christmas postcard signed with Mickey's wavery hand arrived at Walthamstow, nine months after it was sent, and a year and seven months since his last letter on board ship. Wynne was jubilant, her faith was vindicated—she'd known all along he was still alive!

NOTE. The particulars inserted on the address
side and the message in the space below, must
be TYPED or written clearly in BLOCK letters.
MESSAGES MUST NOT BE LONGER THAN 25 WORDS.

23 OCTOBER 1943

DEAREST,

A POSTCARD CAME — AFTER SO LONG WITHOUT
A WORD! I <u>KNEW</u> YOU WERE ALIVE! MY BEST
BOY, AREN'T I THE LUCKIEST, LUCKIEST
GIRL?

      YOUR DEVOTED WIFE,
      WYNNE

25th December

Darling,
My health is excellent.
I am constantly thinking of you. It will be
wonderful when we meet again. Goodbye. God Bless
you. I am waiting for your reply earnestly. Keep
smiling. Don't worry and please give my love to all
at home. All my love. Reply by postcard.

Harold H. Brooks

In the Ferry Boat hotel friends and family celebrated and sang and toasted his health. In the jungles of Java, feverishly dreaming of lilacs amidst the stench and cramps of dysentery, Mickey was dying.

13 November 1943

Darling
We at home are all well. Now I know how to
contact you I can wait more patiently. Did you
receive my letters?

> I love you,
> Wynne

18 Dec 1943

Dearest,
I do hope you are keeping well. I could tell you so
much but 'I love you' is all I have room for.

> *Merry Christmas Darling,*
> *Your Wynne*

The Red Cross prisoner-of-war post provided Wynne with official postcards, and despite the limitations imposed on her messages, the exciting notion that Mickey was alive and would be hearing from her gave her a new zest for life. Ironically, then, the last couple of years of the war were a little easier for her.

1944

16 January 1944

Darling,
Wish I could have some of the warm weather
you must have there. All is well here, but cold.
I LOVE YOU!

> *Your Devoted Wife*
> *Wynne*

18 March 1944

Happy Birthday Darling!
Last year I wrote you a poem. I still have it
for you in case you didn't receive it. Keep well,
my love,

> *Your loving*
> *Wynne*

May 1st 1944

Dearest,
I do hope you are keeping well. All at home are
fine. I miss you more each day. My every thought
is of you.

I love you.
Your Devoted Wynne

Life in England was filled with the daily hardships and irritations of wartime shortages. Wynne could live with food rationing, indeed in later, plumper years she joked that a wartime diet was much better for the figure. However, clothing coupons and the scarcity of shoe leather were particularly irksome for young women who took care of their appearance. When a consignment of leather came into a local bootmender's she hurried down with her only remaining smart pair of courts in need of some attention. Returning the next morning, she found the shop bombed out and her precious shoes blasted with dozens of others into the gutter. Everyone was tired and jaded, but fortunes had changed for the Allies and there was the hint of a new measure of optimism on the streets. Wynne and Vi managed a weekend away at Exmouth in Devon. Like all wartime holidays it had its trials.

After standing in the train for hours, squeezed among men and women in uniform on forty-eight-hour passes and trying to perch on their upturned suitcases, Wynne and Vi managed to miss their destination. All the station signs had been removed long ago in case of invasion. When they eventually arrived at their Exmouth guesthouse the two friends found the rooms damp and the food worse than home. They hadn't been informed that they must bring their own sheets and spent a scratchy night in wool blankets. Nevertheless, Wynne felt able to laugh at inconveniences; they sat in sunshine on the beach between the coils of barbed wire and tasted hope on the salty breeze.

July 21 1944

Darling
Had a funny weekend with Vi in Devon—my
first holiday since you left. Awful lodgings but we
laughed a lot. I long to laugh with you.

Love You,
Wynne

September 21st 1944

Dearest,
So few words but enough to say I love you and
know we shall be together soon. Your Dad has
lumbago but not serious.

   LOVE YOU
   Wynne

1st November 1944

Darling
I'm with my own parents at Laindon, but our little
home ready for you. I long for another postcard—
it's been a year!

> Love you so much,
> Wynne

1945

1st January 1945

Dearest,
Still waiting for news, but at least I know how to
contact you. We toasted the New Year with your
name on our lips.

      Your loving
      Wynne

The summer of 1944 had seen the advent of the 'doodlebugs', Hitler's flying bombs, which wreaked new havoc on London. Wynne finally grew weary of moving her office to and from the air-raid shelter.

2nd March 1945

My Darling,
I'm now a telephone operator for the Civil Service.
I needed a change and I am keeping safe—keep safe
for me.

Your Devoted Wife,
Wynne

April 16th 1945

Darling,
When you come home we'll have a long holiday.
John said he'd treat us to a world tour. Then we
laughed—you've probably done with the world!

   I dream of you,
   Wynne

The war ended in Europe on May 8th and Wynne was celebrating on the streets along with the rest of Britain, despite grey skies and drizzling rain. She joined the rejoicing crowds in Piccadilly where uniformed servicemen were carried on the shoulders of the revellers.

9th May 1945

Darling,
It's over in Europe—nearly there, don't give up!
The streetlights were switched back on last night—
it's like fairyland!

> I love and wait impatiently for you,
> Your Girl

For those with loved ones in Japan's theatre of war, however, the waiting continued. Nevertheless, the prevailing mood was optimistic. The end would come, and at least, Wynne felt, Mickey was away from the fighting.

25th June 1945

Dearest,
Am looking forward to seeing you very soon now!
Remember I love you, Darling, and am only living
for your return.

Your Devoted, Adoring Wife,
Wynne

August 15th, and Japan surrendered at last. Street parties were held all over England, where jellies, tinned salmon and other apparently impossible, hoarded treats emerged from the back of larders. Euphoric, Wynne abandoned the dreary prisoner-of-war postcards. Confident that RAF Records would be able to reach Mickey, she joyfully returned to her letters.

20th August 1945

My Own Dearest
At last this horrible business is over! We've been
celebrating for days, everyone is so excited at the
thought of seeing you again—especially me! It's
been so awful without you. My whole life stopped
still the day you went away. Just as one finds it
difficult to move one's limbs after a heavy sleep, so
my heart finds it difficult to beat again now that
I know you are coming home.

I'm going back to Preston Road and I shall make
our little home so beautiful for you, we'll never
want to leave it again! I can't believe I've had to
wait nearly two years without a word since your
postcard. But now you'll be able to write. Write
soon, my love, and tell me when I can expect you
home and rush into your arms!

1945

Your VERY *Devoted and* ALWAYS
Adoring Wife,

Wynne

xxxxxxxxxxxxxxxxxxxxxxxxxxx

xxxxxxxxxxxxxxxxxxxxxxxxxxx

xxxxxxxxxxxxxx

Although rumours were rife, it wasn't until after the camps began to be liberated that the stories of the terrible conditions there began to emerge. Wynne learnt of the starvation and torture and tried to imagine its effect on Mickey.

September 6th 1945

Oh My Angel
I know things have been so hard for you and you
have to recover from your ordeal. I promise I won't
rush you, I know it won't be easy for you. We'll
take things very quietly at first and get you strong
again. I hope you don't find me changed. Sometimes
I look in the mirror and think I look so much older
than I did when you went away; and thinner,
too—we'll have to build up our strength together!
You know I'll always be your sweetheart and you
mine, no matter how careworn we are and even
when we're old and grey. You used to call me your
enchantress—well I shall work my magic and
make all your suffering vanish away, just you wait
and see.

Every day without you is agony, but I'm also joyful because I know our bad, dark times are almost over and I shall be with my own love soon,

Your loving, loving, loving
Wynne

x x x x x x x x x x x

Throughout September and October, Wynne was preparing for Mickey's return; excited, nervous, and with the confidence of the young that she could cope with any residual traumas connected with his ordeal. News of survivors trickled through and she expected to hear of him any day, as she cleaned and recleaned the house in readiness.

By November the old fear had returned. The icy and familiar serpent constricted her heart and watched with her for the morning post. First, the letters were returned—all of them—unopened, unread. The comfort they contained was undelivered, the envelopes marked 'Return to Sender, No Trace, RAF India Command'.

November 1945

Darling Heart,
I wrote dozens of letters to you and they've all been
returned. It's so dreadful that you never received
anything from me, but I have them all here for you
to read. I hope this will get through. I'm so worried
that I haven't heard from you and the War over
three months. I've read about the terrible things that
happened in those camps. Oh my dear love, I pray
and pray that you haven't suffered too much, but
soon you'll be home and I'll make it up to you.
I wish I could hear something from you. Perhaps
you're on a hospital ship with loss of memory.
I really don't care what state you are in as long as
you are here with me. I hope it will be soon. I went
up to town with Doreen today and bought a cherry-
coloured coat. I think you will like it—I shall
wear it when I come to meet you. Poor Doreen lost
her Stanley at El Alamein. You don't know how

*I've dreaded the telegram boy, my love. And now
I'm still waiting for news. I love you, come home
to me.*

Wynne

dear heart

EPITAPH TO A LOVER

I remember the way you smiled at me across a room, as though no-one else existed. I remember your hand on my knee, and your smooth, cool fingers stroking my skin. My mind is smudged with memories and just when I think my heart can't break any more, it does. But you'll always be there at the centre of my being, whatever happens, until the end. And then you'll be waiting for me. Until then,

> *Farewell my love*
> *Wynne*

Sid endured the last part of the war at Cycle Camp, Java among 5000 Allied prisoners. Men were constantly sick; the camp desperately over-crowded. Over six foot in height, when liberated Sid weighed less than five stone. Recuperation took place on a hospital ship in Australian waters. Sydney Harbour, he thought, looked dazzling, but he was never able to go ashore. The Red Cross gave him a sack of letters from his mother, withheld by the Japanese, and gradually he reacquainted himself with his former life as he regained strength. Bouts of malaria subsided. The night-mares, however, never went away.

1946

A suburban London street under a February frost, the windows watchful, suspicious. A gaunt young man, stepping cautiously on the slippery pavement, hesitates before the first gate in the street. The creak as it opens seems so loud in the still air. The curtains move as he walks the short path through the sleeping garden. There are the lilacs, black and lifeless, waiting for warmth and hope before they can be regenerated. He lifts the frozen knocker. A woman opens the door.

He gave her the wristwatch before either of them spoke. There was no mistaking her, of course. He'd fallen in love with her in the camp; Mickey's stories had sustained them both. She didn't move—he must have done it all wrong. Perhaps he shouldn't have come.

She spoke so softly he hardly heard her.

'Hello Sid.' She was crying.

So was he.

For her, it was a gradual thawing. In the garden

the first green shoots appeared. Rain softened the earth, blackbirds sang in the lilac trees. Within, her private frost receded. Here was a connection between her old life and a chance at a new.

POST OFFICE

TELEGRAM

WEST LONDON

AUG 16TH 47

WYNNE BROOKS 9 THE VINES CLARENDON RD
WOODFORD E18

MANY HAPPY RETURNS OF TOMORROW SWEET.
MAY YOU SEE MANY WONDERFUL TIMES.

MUCH LOVE, SID

Uncle Sid and Aunt Wynne—some years later they were married, and their union, though childless, was a happy one. How could it not be, so capable of love and laughter as they both were? Sid's optimism allowed him to recover slowly from his experiences, and he and his brother took over their father's gentlemen's outfitters business in Pentonville Road. In their later years, Sid and Wynne sat around the fire with their comical, spoilt dog and told their nieces of their escapades at evening classes, their visits to Paris to practise their new skills with the French language, their fun with amateur dramatics. Wynne told us of Sid's foray into pantomime—dancing in *Aladdin and his Lamp* with the ladies of the harem, not one of them under fifty-five, and he blacked up with boot polish. They scrubbed and scrubbed to remove it but he was still left with a ring around his neck and black in his eyebrows and under his nails—Wynne made him wear gloves when they went to church next day in case he had to shake hands with the vicar. And then they laughed so much they couldn't tell us any more

Laughing and crying, good times and bad— Wynne, Mickey and Sid had their share of both, but laughter was triumphant. Sid and Wynne preferred to recall for us the good times. Good memories, they said, nourish the soul.